AF261055

Our Young Voices

2016

Scholarship Week
Cleveland, Ohio

Banquet
College Fair
Our Young Voices Dream Contest

Contest Winners
• Jamel Clayton • Taliaha Ward • Jibrael Harris •

Our Young Voices 2016, AAMA, Cleveland Infinite Scholars Week © 2016 by Universal Prosperity, Jamel Clayton, Taliaha Ward, Jibrael Harris.

All rights reserved. Printed in the United States of America. No part of this book may be used or reproduced in any manner whatsoever without written permission except in the case of brief quotations embodied in critical articles or reviews.

This book is a work of non-fiction. However, names, characters, businesses, organizations, places, events and incidents either are the product of the author's imagination or are used fictitiously. Any resemblance to actual persons, living or dead, events, or locales is entirely coincidental.

For information contact: info@uptownmediaventures.com

Book and Cover design by Team Uptown

ISBN: 978-1-68121-047-6

10 9 8 7 6 5 4 3 2 1

Dedicated to enabling youth the experience of expressing themselves with the written word and the

Pride In Authorship!

INFINITE
SCHOLARS
"The Possibilities are Infinite"

Table of Contents

Board Chair Preface   7

Introduction   9

Endorsements   11

The 2016 AAMA Fifth Annual
    Scholarship Week Banquet,
    Cleveland, Ohio   19

The 2016, Infinite Scholars College Fair,
    Cleveland, Ohio   37

The 2016, AAMA and Our Young Voices
    Dream Contest
    Cleveland, Ohio   49

Participating Colleges and Universities   63

Summary Report   75

Board Chair Preface

As the Director of Public Information for the Cleveland Fire Department, I have been involved in many public service activities that benefit the public at large. I have always had a keen desire to positively influence our youth – the future of our society.

As fortuity would have it, I was presented with the idea of starting an initiative for the benefit of our youth. The initiative, ultimately, became the *Pride in Authorship Initiative*. The folks at a small publishing house, *Uptown Media Joint Ventures*, committed to insure the publication of a semi-annual book called *Our Young Voices.*

After much behind the scenes preparation, I am proud to announce the successful publication of a second volume of *Our Young Voices,* in conjunction with the African American Music Association during the Scholarship Week in conjunction with Infinite Scholars.

This is surely just the beginning and we thank all of our sponsors, supporters, and everyone who has contributed to this extremely worthwhile initiative. So please join us, as we celebrate our young essayists who have earned the right to claim the *Pride in Authorship!*

Larry Gray

Board Chairman, Universal Prosperity, Pride in Authorship Initiative

K Kelly with Winston Gragg, President of the African American Music Association and Member of the Infinite Scholars Board of Directors

Introduction

How many people can claim to be published authors as youths?

The *Our Young Voices* publication is one of the manifestations of the *Pride In Authorship Initiative* that seeks to promote written expression by our youth.

Another part of this initiative is the participation in *Youth Literary and Writing Contests*. The winning essays will be published in the *Our Young Voices* publication, with the winner's photo (if available at printing time), and available on major book retailing web sites like Amazon.com and Barnes & Noble.com. Each winner will receive a free copy of their book, an award certification of authorship, along with other prizes!

Yet, ultimately, the greatest reward is seeing their beaming *Pride In Authorship*!

K Kelly McElroy

Executive Director, Universal Prosperity
CEO, Uptown Media Joint Ventures
Author, Best of the Best, Modern Jazz Recordings

Winston Gragg

President African American Music Association and Member of the Infinite Scholars Board of Directors

"My idea for being involved with *Our Young Voices* is to make a concentrated effort to helping young people and re-educating adults about today's marketplace. Many adults are afraid of technology, however, our children are not. Walt Disney prepares young children to go to Disney, and we want to prepare kids in elementary and middle school to go to college to get an education. In order to teach young people, you have to get their attention, and that is exactly what *Our Young Voices* is doing."

Dimitrios Kalafatis

Special Events Coordinator
Golden Corral

"Children are our future and I am, personally, proud to support such worthy causes and programs such as Infinite Scholars and the *Our Young Voices* initiative. Golden Corral is committed to the improvement of society-at-large by supporting such noteworthy civic organizations and programs."

EB Smith

M.P.A., Author, Educator
Media Associate for the
African American Music Association
Vice President, E.B. Smith Project LLC

"Higher education helps develop a person's inner gifts. Student's minds are sharpened with the knowledge and critical thinking skills necessary to compete. I am pleased to be involved with the African American Music Association of Cleveland, Ohio and their continued effort in providing access for young people to get to college. I also support the efforts of *Our Young Voices* in promoting literary expression among our youth. My life serves as proof that their life will be better with it."

Jean Wilson

Executive Administrator
African American Music Association

"Our Young Voices gives children and teens an opportunity to express their idea in a public forum. It teaches them how to communicate both written and verbally. Developing these skills at an early age also helps young people to build high self-esteem as well as interpersonal (dealing with others) and intrapersonal communication skills. Students also learn key competencies such as: the ability to solve problems, how to control thoughts and actions, use of critical thinking skills, and the ability to motivate others. We are really excited about the *Our Young Voices* program, because it is making a difference in young people's lives."

The 2016 AAMA Fifth Annual Scholarship Week Banquet Cleveland, Ohio

The Banquet was held Thursday, September 8, 2016. The Annual Scholarship Banquet and Community Service Awards Reception was honored to have the support of both City of Cleveland Councilman, Kevin Conwell, and Mrs. Yvonne Conwell, Cuyahoga County Council Representative. The event took place at the Tudor Arms Hotel.

Special Guest Speakers for the evening were Mike Tobin, Public Information Officer, U.S. Attorney from the United States Attorney's Office for the Northern District of Ohio. Also, Felton Thomas, Director of the Cleveland Public Library.

Distinguished invited guests included Mr. and Mrs. Carl S. Ewing, President of the Association of the African American Cultural Garden and others.

Other highlights included a Community Service Award presentation to the following individuals who have dedicated their life to work and service in the community:

Derrick Polk – Polk played basketball with Ohio State University and The Harlem Globe Trotters as well as playing overseas.

Emanuel Leaks – Leaks played basketball for six pro seasons with four different ABA teams and a pair of NBA clubs. In 2004 Leaks was also Inducted into the Greater Cleveland Sports Hall Of Fame.

(Mike Tobin, U.S. Attorney's Office top right, bottom)

(Felton Thomas, Director of the Cleveland Public Library)

(State of Ohio Representative, 12th District, John Barnes, Jr. top left)

(Lynn Hampton, President, Black Shield)

(Emanuel Leaks, former pro player, ABA and NBA basketball)

(Derrick Polk, former Globe Trotter and overseas basketball player)

(Cierra Kelley, Cleveland School District top; Sonja Saalam, bottom)

(Kevin Conwell & Footprint Band)

(Kevin Conwell & Footprint Band)

(Yvonne Conwell, Cuyahoga County Representative, top middle, bottom left)

(Kevin Conwell, Cleveland City Councilman, top right, bottom right)

(Carl and Lavita Ewing, President and Development Chairperson,
The Association of African American Cultural Gardens)

(E.B. Smith, Media Associate for the African American Music Association Vice President, E.B. Smith Project LLC, top ,middle; bottom right)

(Kent & Angelica WERE 1490)

The 2016

Infinite Scholars College Fair
Cleveland, Ohio

The African American Music Association invited high school students and their families to a "FREE" scholarship fair held September 9, 2016. The Infinite Scholars College Scholarship Fair was held at the Martin Luther King, Jr., Cleveland Public Library located at 1962 Stokes Blvd, Cleveland, Ohio 44106.

SEE IF YOU QUALIFY FOR
FULL
POTENTIAL
goarmy.com
Central
State
University

DAY'S FBI.
S FOR YOU.
w.FBIjobs.gov

FISK
UNIVERSITY
FULL
POTENT

(Anthony Battaglia, Cleveland Metropolitan School District)

(Cierra Kelley, Cleveland Metropolitan School District)

(Yvonne Conwell, Cuyahoga County Representative)

(Kevin Conwell, Cleveland City Councilman)

(Winston Gragg, President of the AAMA, top left; bottom, middle. Lynn Hampton, President, Black Shield, top right)

(Jean Wilson, Executive Administrator, AAMA, top right, bottom 2nd from left. Kent & Angelica, WERE 1490)

The 2016

AAMA and Our Young Voices Dream Contest

Cleveland, Ohio

The Our Young Voices, Dream Contest for Middle Schools was held on Saturday, September 10, 2016 at the First Cleveland Mosque.

The winners of the Our Young Voices Dream Contest are:

Jamel Clayton

Taliaha Ward

Jibrael Harris

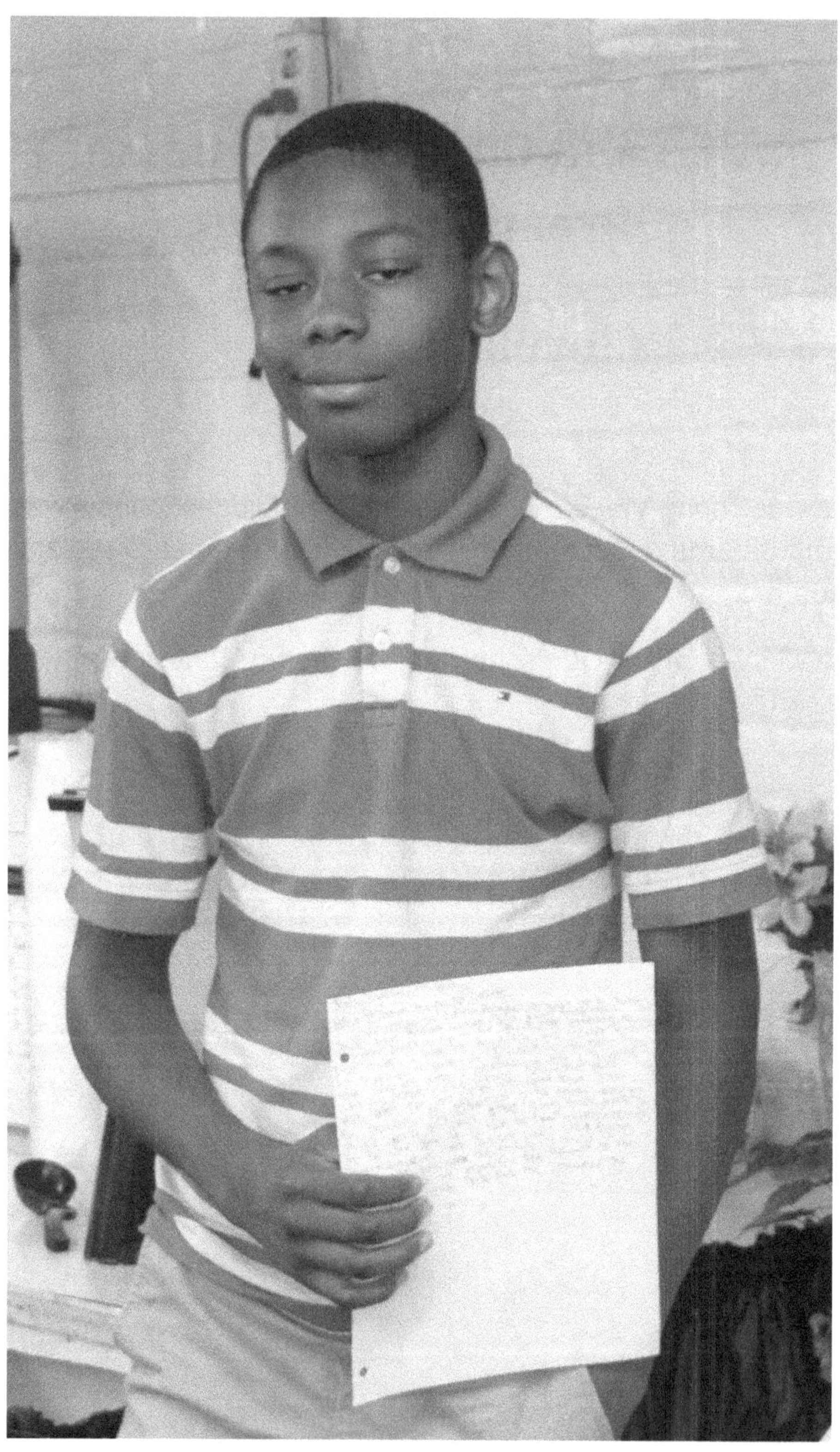

Jamel Clayton

Why I Want To Go To College

I want to go to college because I want to be successful and prove society wrong. As a young black man everything is against us. I have something to prove to myself. I have to be a leader and encouragement to my community and race. I want to go to the Marines, then I want to go to college. I want to get my masters and doctorate degrees. I want everyone to see that I am independent and that I can be successful. My education is the most important thing in my life. I want other young Blacks to do the same and to have the same mind-set, persistence, and determination. A house divided can't stand. Divided we fall. Abraham Lincoln wrote with unity there is strength, united we stand for the strength of the wolf is the pack and the strength of the pack is the wolf.

Talaiha Ward

Why I Want To Go To College

I want to go to college because I want to get a good education. An education will benefit me in multiple ways. People with an education tend to get better jobs than people without an education.

Another reason I would like to go to college is because I want to set an example for my younger siblings. My younger siblings look up to me. If I don't go to college, there is a 64% chance they won't either.

I also want to go to college to pursue my career as a neurosurgeon. To become a neurosurgeon, I have to go to college for six to eight years. If I don't go to college, this won't happen.

Also, I would make more money going to college. I want to make enough to afford my own house, car, bills, and essentials for my family. And maybe build my own hospital someday.

There are excellent reasons to go to college including: to get an education, to be an example for someone that looks up to you, to get the job that you want instead of flipping burgers, and to make enough money to live long and prosper.

Jibreal Harris

Why I Want To Go To College

Going to college is important to me because it is a way to make my dreams come true. I dream of becoming a commercial pilot. I want to fly all over the world. I want to see different places and meet different people. When I see planes flying over me I think that, 'someday I will fly one of those.' To travel to different places and to see the world would be very expensive but if you are a pilot you get paid to see all these great places. Going to college and studying aviation for four years will help me become a pilot. When I am at college I will have flight training to help me get the flight certificates and training that I will need. Even though no college is required to be a pilot, I think it is important to have a college degree.

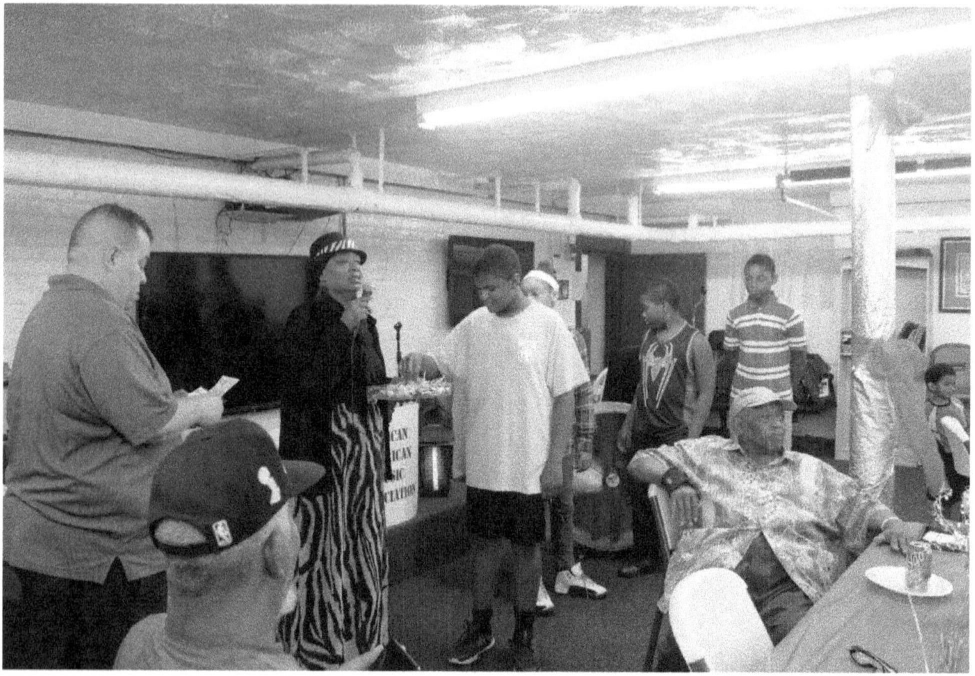

(Dimitrios Kalafatis, Special events Marketing Coordinator,
Golden Corral, top left; bottom, left)

(Imam Abbas, top; and Jean Wilson, AAMA, bottom)

SHARP

ARMY STRONG

Participating Universities and Colleges

The University of Akron
Army ROTC

ASHLAND
UNIVERSITY

BETHUNE-COOKMAN

BW
BALDWIN
WALLACE
UNIVERSITY

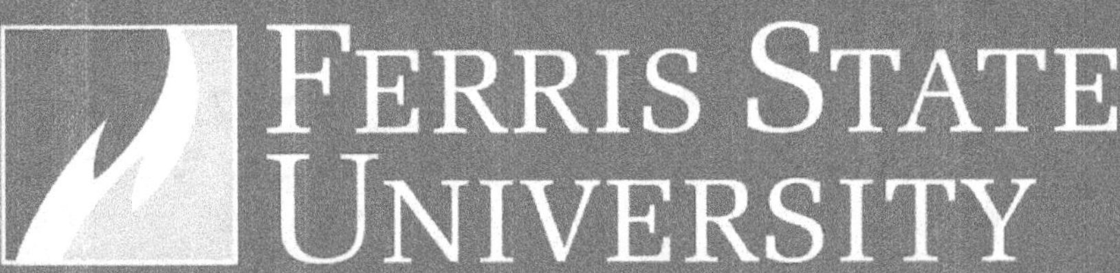

FERRIS STATE
UNIVERSITY

FISK
UNIVERSITY
established Nashville, TN 1866

HAMPTON
UNIVERSITY
THE STANDARD OF EXCELLENCE

John Carroll
UNIVERSITY

SIGILLUM · COLLEGII · LACUS · ERIENSIS
Ps. XC. 17.
1856
LAKE ERIE
COLLEGE

THE
LINCOLN
UNIVERSITY
1854

MOUNT UNION
COLLEGE

NSU
NORFOLK STATE UNIVERSITY
RMU
ROBERT MORRIS™

SHAW UNIVERSITY

WAYNESBURG
UNIVERSITY

WestVirginiaUniversity

WILBERFORCE
UNIVERSITY

Youngstown
STATE UNIVERSITY

Summary Report

Cleveland Student Attendance in 2012 was 64 students and attendance in 2013 was 122 students.

Cleveland - (September 12, 2014)

Students	141
Parents/Teachers	19
Colleges	21
Awards	$705,000

Cleveland - (September 11, 2015)

Students	235
Parents	31
Colleges	24
Awards	$1,224,350

Cleveland - (September 09, 2016)

Students	160
Parents	31
Colleges	32
Awards	$2,000,000

A Proud Supporter of:

OUR YOUNG VOICES IS A PRIDE IN AUTHORSHIP INITIA-
TIVE PUBLICATION. THE YOUNG AUTHORS SELECTED
HAVE SUCCESSFULLY CONVEYED THEIR THOUGHTS,
DREAMS, AND CONCERNS BY THE WRITTEN WORD.
THEY DESERVE TO BE CELEBRATED!

During the past decade, the Infinite Scholars Program has served more than 100,000 students and has facilitated more than 1 Billion Dollars in scholarships and financial aid.

Infinite Scholarship Fairs are located in 27 cities and growing. We connect students with scholarship and financial aid opportunities from participating colleges. There is no cost to students or colleges to attend our fairs.

Nearly 300 colleges and universities annually participate in our scholarship fairs. Each fair hosts between 50 and 100 colleges. Our Featured Colleges provide Infinite Scholars with additional support beyond attending our scholarship fairs.

http://www.infinitescholar.org/

IRON FIST
BOXING
ACADEMY

NOW REGISTERING
ALL AGES ABILITIES SKILL LEVELS
LOSE EXCUSES,
FIND RESULTS.
IRON FIST
BOXING
ACADEMY
3209 Chester Ave. CLE
www.ironfistboxing.com

UNIVERSAL
PROSPERITY
Promoting Business
and Social Unity
NON SECTARIAN
NON POLITICAL

Supporters of Our Young Voices Can get their books published and keep 100% control and profits of their book for only $250!

Mention "Our Young Voices" on the "Contact Us" Page or VIA E-Mail

Easy Self-Publishing

http://uptownmediaventures.com

(Click the Publishing Page)

Forward E-Mail Inquiries to:

uptownliterary@gmail.com

Our Young Voices

2016

Scholarship Week

Cleveland, Ohio

Banquet
College Fair
Our Young Voices Dream Contest

Contest Winners
· Jamel Clayton · Taliaha Ward · Jibrael Harris ·

www.ingramcontent.com/pod-product-compliance
Lightning Source LLC
Chambersburg PA
CBHW080307030726
47593CB00009B/2672